BIOGRAPHY FROM
ANCIENT CIVILIZATIONS
LEGENDS, FOLKLORE, AND STORIES OF ANCIENT WORLDS

The Life and Times of

PLATO

Mitchell Lane
PUBLISHERS

P.O. Box 196
Hockessin, Delaware 19707

BIOGRAPHY FROM
ANCIENT CIVILIZATIONS
LEGENDS, FOLKLORE, AND STORIES OF ANCIENT WORLDS

Titles in the Series

The Life and Times of

BIOGRAPHY FROM
ANCIENT CIVILIZATIONS
LEGENDS, FOLKLORE, AND STORIES OF ANCIENT WORLDS

The Life and Times of

PLATO

Jim Whiting

Mitchell Lane
PUBLISHERS

Printing   2   3   4   5   6   7   8   9

Library of Congress Cataloging-in-Publication Data
Whiting, Jim, 1943–
    The life and times of Plato / by Jim Whiting.
       p. cm. — (Biography from ancient civilizations)
    Includes bibliographical references and index.
    ISBN 1-58415-507-8 (library bound : alk. paper)
    1. Plato—Juvenile literature. 2. Philosophers—Greece—Biography—Juvenile literature. 3. Greece—History—To 146 B.C.—Juvenile literature. I. Title. II. Series.
B393.W45 2006
184—dc22
                                                   2005036689

ISBN-13: 978-1-58415-507-2

ABOUT THE AUTHOR: Jim Whiting has been a remarkably versatile and accomplished journalist, writer, editor, and photographer for more than 30 years. A voracious reader since early childhood, Mr. Whiting has written and edited about 200 nonfiction children's books. His subjects range from authors to zoologists and include contemporary pop icons and classical musicians, saints and scientists, emperors and explorers. Representative titles include *The Life and Times of Franz Liszt*, *The Life and Times of Julius Caesar*, *Charles Schulz*, *Charles Darwin and the Origin of the Species*, and *Juan Ponce de Leon*.

    Other career highlights are a lengthy stint publishing *Northwest Runner*, the first piece of original fiction to appear in *Runners World* magazine, hundreds of descriptions and venue photographs for America Online, e-commerce product writing, sports editor for the *Bainbridge Island Review*, light verse in a number of magazines, and acting as the official photographer for the Antarctica Marathon.

    He lives in Washington State with his wife and two teenage sons.

PHOTO CREDITS: Cover, pp. 1, 3, 41—Superstock; p. 6—Time Life Pictures/Getty Images; p. 14—Hulton Archive/Getty Images; p. 19—World Maps; pp. 24, 30—Sharon Beck; p. 20—Barbara McManus/London British Museum; pp. 33, 39—Jamie Kondrchek; p. 36—Picture Post/Getty Images; p. 38—Ancient Greek Men.

PUBLISHER'S NOTE: This story is based on the author's extensive research, which he believes to be accurate. Documentation of such research is contained on page 47.

    The internet sites referenced herein were active as of the publication date. Due to the fleeting nature of some web sites, we cannot guarantee they will all be active when you are reading this book.

    To reflect current usage, we have chosen to use the secular era designations BCE ("before the common era") and CE ("of the common era") instead of the traditional designations BC ("before Christ") and AD (*anno Domini*, "in the year of the Lord").

The Life and Times of

PLATO

*For Your Information

Plato, above, was a devoted student of Socrates. No one is sure what Plato actually looked like. This image was made about 2,000 years after his death. It shows Plato delivering a point about his philosophical views.

CHAPTER ONE

SENTENCED TO DIE

There's nothing like a juicy celebrity trial to get people talking. In recent years, nearly everyone had an opinion about the guilt or innocence of high-profile defendants such as Michael Jackson, Martha Stewart, and Congressman Tom DeLay. Two thousand years ago, Jesus of Nazareth went on trial before Roman governor Pontius Pilate. His is probably the most famous trial in world history.

About four hundred years before Jesus was sentenced to die on the cross, a notorious legal case rocked the city of Athens, Greece.

The trial centered on one of its most famous citizens, the philosopher Socrates. He had been a popular teacher for decades. Many people who witnessed the proceedings, including Plato, had studied with him. He was a recognized war hero. Then, at the age of seventy, he was hauled into court.

He was facing two very serious charges. One was impiety. His accusers said that Socrates didn't believe in the gods that were sacred to Athens. The other charge was that he corrupted the city's youth.

The ancient Greeks believed in gods who were quick to administer punishment at the slightest offense. These gods were well known for their jealousy. Everyone believed that the gods didn't just retaliate against the individual who offended them. They took out their anger on the entire population. If Socrates offended the gods, all of Athens would be in danger.

Corrupting the youth was also serious. Allegedly, Socrates was filling the heads of young people with bad ideas. The Athenians didn't have to look very far for "evidence." Several of Socrates' former students had done things that threatened the city's democratic ideals. There was no proof that Socrates had done anything to encourage them in their treasonous deeds. It didn't matter. It was a case of guilt by association.

Many of the trial procedures of ancient Greece were similar to those of today. Socrates' trial began when a citizen named Meletus made an accusation against Socrates. Any citizen of Athens had that right. Both Socrates and Meletus appeared a few days later before the city's chief magistrate, a man similar to a judge. The magistrate listened as both men presented their sides. He decided that the lawsuit Meletus brought was acceptable under Athenian law.

The next step was a preliminary hearing. Meletus presented a written summary of his charges. Socrates responded. The magistrate questioned each man. Socrates and Meletus also questioned each other. The magistrate considered both sides. He determined that the case should go to trial.

The trial took place in the Agora, the public marketplace of Athens. A jury of 500 men listened to the case. The large size was intentional. Small juries were subject to bribery. It would be impossible to buy off such a large group. In addition to the huge jury, it is likely that hundreds of citizens packed the Agora.

Unlike modern-day trials, in ancient Athens there were no attorneys. The trial lasted one day. The sentence was carried out right away. And there were no appeals.

But there was one very strong similarity with modern-day court cases. Many people had already made up their minds about Socrates' guilt or innocence before the trial began. Many if not most of Socrates' students liked and respected him, but he was not universally popular in the city. That's not unusual. Even today, there are very few public figures who don't have their share of enemies. That was certainly the case with Socrates.

Athens in his day was very prosperous. Many of its inhabitants were trying to "get ahead in life." Socrates wasn't. His only concern was the life of the mind. He lived at a near-poverty level. Many of his fellow citizens didn't understand him. People often fear people they don't understand. Others thought he was just being lazy.

The playwright Aristophanes was one of the city's most famous comedy writers. He didn't like Socrates. He wrote a play called *The Clouds* that focuses on Socrates. According to Aristophanes, Socrates runs a "school" called The Thinkery. He teaches anything that people will pay him to teach. He is especially successful at making a bad argument sound good. That Socrates was an especially ugly man gave Aristophanes another avenue for his comedy. The mask that the character playing Socrates wore exaggerated the philosopher's looks. People laughed when they saw it.

Some of the additional laughs came from Aristophanes' use of bathroom humor. One character tells another that Socrates wanted to know if a fly makes noise through its mouth or its anus. According to the first character, Socrates has discovered "the gastric gas of the gnat is forced under pressure down to the rump. At that point the compressed gases, as through a narrow valve, escape with a whoosh, thereby causing the characteristic tootle or cry of the flatulent gnat."

"So the gnat has a bugle up its [butt]!" the other character replies. "Why, the man who has mastered the [butt] of the gnat could win an acquittal from any court."[1]

The first character adds that Socrates was cheated out of making an important scientific discovery about the orbit of the moon. "There he stood, gaping open-mouthed at the sky, when a lizard on the roof let loose on him." The second character replies, "Ha! A lizard crapping on Socrates! That's rich."[2]

A third exchange ridicules Socrates' teaching methods. A group of students who have been with him for a long time are on their hands and knees. Their foreheads are pressed against the ground. They are doing "research" on what the earth is made of.

The first character asks, "Why are their [butts] scanning the skies?"

The other responds, "Taking a minor in astronomy."[3] In other words, they are "studying" the stars with their rears.

Aristophanes' meaning is clear. Socrates is the kind of man who will do anything to turn a fast buck.

According to some historians, Socrates attended a performance of *The Clouds*. When his character first appeared on stage, Socrates good-naturedly stood up. That way the audience could compare his actual face with the mask the character portraying him was wearing.

Aside from the obvious humor, there was a dark side to the comedy. It wasn't all in fun. It demonstrated that not everyone in Athens approved of Socrates' methods. Many of his supporters believed the play helped to create a climate of opinion against Socrates. More than twenty years after Aristophanes presented his play, this negative opinion allowed Meletus and two other men, Anytus and Lycon, to bring serious charges against him.

As the trial opened, the three accusers had a total of three hours to speak. One at a time, they mounted an elevated stage. A water clock kept track of the time as they provided "evidence" in support of their charges.

Socrates had equal time—three hours—to answer the charges. He began by branding his accusers as liars. He pointed out that he was a first-time offender. He firmly denied the charges, especially that of impiety. He said that the charges cut to the heart of his sense of personal worth.

"Men of Athens, I care for and love you, but I shall obey the god rather than you, and while I have life and strength I shall never cease from the practice and teaching of philosophy . . . [I will always greet anyone] in my usual manner: 'You, my friend—a citizen of the great city of Athens, famous for its culture and power—are you not ashamed of heaping up the largest amount of money and status and reputation, and caring so little about wisdom and truth and improving your soul, which you never regard or heed at all?' "[4]

He concluded, "I do believe that there are gods, and in a sense higher than that in which any of my accusers believe in them."[5]

The case went to the jury. The members didn't spend any time talking among themselves. They began voting immediately. The vote was 280 in favor of conviction, 220 in favor of acquittal.

Then came what is known today as the penalty phase. Socrates' accusers asked for the death penalty. Many scholars consider it likely that the jury didn't want to administer the death penalty. It had lesser options. It could fine Socrates. It could exile him, especially because the margin of conviction was relatively narrow. Exile would serve the primary purpose of the proceedings. Athens would be rid of Socrates.

Socrates had several minutes to persuade the jury to allow him to live. Many people in his position would have pleaded for forgiveness. Not Socrates. First he said that he was one of the most valuable citizens of Athens because he was trying to bring out the good in everyone to whom he spoke. He said that he fully intended to go on doing the same thing.

"What would be a reward suitable to a poor man who is your benefactor, and who needs leisure to devote to instructing you?" he asked.

He answered his own question. "There could be no reward more fitting for such a man than to be given free meals . . . for life."[6]

He concluded on what seems like a more serious note. He suggested a fine. He didn't have any money himself. He guaranteed that his friends and supporters would pay the fine for him.

The jury voted for the death penalty. Reportedly the margin was considerably higher than the vote to convict. Even then, Socrates was defiant. First he chided them for hastening his death. Old age would have solved their "problem" within a few years. Then he said, "[I do not] repent of the style of my defense; I would rather die having spoken in my manner than live in the manner you like."[7]

His friends tried to save him from his fate. He could have escaped from Athens relatively easily. He chose not to. He said that the jury had made a mistake in convicting him. On the other hand, he believed that the jury system was a recognized part of the government of Athens. Socrates had always supported the government, and he felt it was his obligation to respect its decision. To escape would have been dishonorable.

Typically, Socrates spent his final hours on earth in a philosophical discussion with his friends. "Seeing all these things, what ought not we to do in order to obtain virtue and wisdom in this life? Fair is the prize, and the hope great!"[8] he concluded.

The time had come. Socrates took a bath, said good-bye to his wife and children, then drank a cup of hemlock, a poison. His friends began crying. Socrates scolded them.

"What is this strange outcry?" he said. "I sent away the women mainly in order that they might not offend in this way, for I have heard that a man should die in peace. Be quiet, then, and have patience."[9]

Soon the poison began its deadly work. First his feet, then his legs, then his stomach became numb. Socrates pulled a blanket over his face. A few more minutes passed. Someone picked up the blanket. Socrates was dead.

Socrates

While few actual details of his life have been established, some things are known about Socrates. He said he was 70 at the time of his trial in 399, so he was probably born in 469 or 470 BCE. There is evidence that his father was Sophroniscus and his mother was Phaenarete. His father was a stoneworker, someone who helps with construction projects. Many scholars believe that Socrates worked for his father for a while. The business must have been prosperous. He joined the heavy infantry of Athens. These soldiers were called hoplites. They had to provide their own body armor and weapons. This gear was expensive. Only well-to-do citizens could afford it.

Almost nothing is known about the first half of his life. In particular, how he came to be so interested in philosophy is a mystery.

He eventually married a woman named Xantippe, though the wedding date is unknown. It may have been relatively late in his life. At the time of his trial, he had three children. All were sons. Two of them were still fairly young.

Xantippe reputedly had a bad temper. The family's financial circumstances probably added to her grumpy attitude. Socrates didn't charge money for his teaching. The family lived near the poverty level.

The outbreak of the Peloponnesian War in 431 BCE provides some information about Socrates. Plato mentions his military service during the conflict several times. These include his heroism and his ability to withstand suffering. Greece in winter can be very cold. Socrates wore only thin clothing and went barefoot while he was on duty.

Athenians had cause to distrust him in the final years of the war. Some former students led a revolt against the city's democratic government in 411. In 406, Athens put several naval commanders on trial together. Under Athenian law, they should have been tried as individuals. Socrates opposed the trial because it was illegal. Athens overruled him. In 404 BCE another revolt resulted in numerous deaths. Suddenly Socrates didn't seem like a harmless old man anymore. Many important people wanted to get rid of him. Five years later they would have their chance.

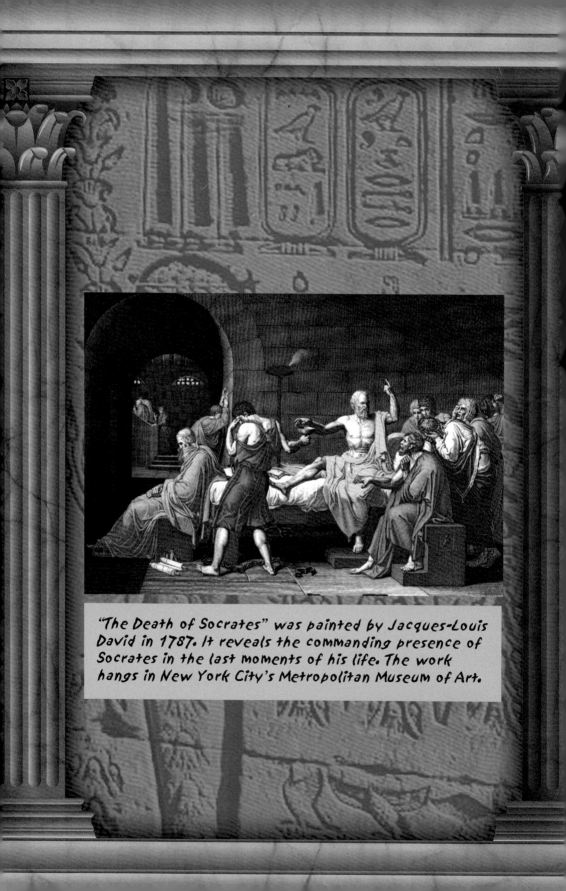

"The Death of Socrates" was painted by Jacques-Louis David in 1787. It reveals the commanding presence of Socrates in the last moments of his life. The work hangs in New York City's Metropolitan Museum of Art.

CHAPTER
TWO

GROWING UP A THINKER

Many details of Socrates' trial and execution have been debated for centuries. Other details are certain: Socrates was tried and convicted of the two charges. There is general agreement about the margin of votes that were cast for conviction and for the death penalty. His death resulted from his drinking hemlock.

There are only two surviving records about the actual proceedings. Both were written by young men who had been his students. Both men greatly admired him. This admiration could have colored their accounts of the trial and its aftermath.

One man was Xenophon. He later participated in an expedition of thousands of Greek soldiers into Asia. They were cut off. Their leaders were murdered, yet most of the men returned. Xenophon became famous for writing *Anabasis*, a book about their experiences during the long and difficult homeward march. He referred to the men as the Ten Thousand.

The other was Plato. He became famous for writing about philosophy. Today, many people believe that philosophy doesn't have anything to do with daily life. Few people study philosophy in college. They choose to study something more "useful."

The Greeks felt very differently about philosophy. It was integral to their daily lives. They believed that philosophy could help them determine what was right and wrong.

To Plato, Socrates' execution was unjust. It was probably the most important event in his life. The shock of seeing Athens' democratic government execute his beloved teacher convinced him that democracy was a terrible form of government.

It also convinced him that it was absolutely essential to preserve the memory of Socrates. Socrates had spent nearly all his time teaching. He didn't write down any of his ideas. Plato already had some experience as a writer. He had written some poetry. Socrates disapproved of poetry, so Plato had stopped writing it.

After Socrates died, Plato resumed his writing—but he didn't write poetry. He wrote a series of stories in which Socrates is the central character. These stories take the form of dialogues. In each dialogue, Socrates has a conversation with one or more prominent Athenians. The participants in the dialogues discuss important issues—what is the right way to behave, what is beautiful, what is the best method of government, and more.

In most of the dialogues, Socrates doesn't talk about his ideas. In fact, he says that he doesn't have any ideas. The other participants in the dialogues all have ideas. Socrates asks them what they think. His questioning brings out the fact that in nearly every case, their ideas have serious weaknesses. They are incorrect. He believes it is only by carefully examining incorrect ideas that it is possible to arrive at the truth.

Plato succeeded in his intention. His dialogues preserved the name and the fame of Socrates. In fact, he went far beyond his original plan. Socrates never organized his thoughts into a system of philosophy. Plato did it for him. As he continued to write his dialogues, he began using Socrates to express his own ideas about philosophy.

Scholars divide Plato's dialogues into three groups: early, middle, and late. They believe that the early dialogues are reasonably accurate in showing what Socrates thought. *The Apology* was probably the first dialogue Plato wrote. It is Plato's record of the trial. The title might make us think that Socrates was saying he was sorry. That isn't the case. In Plato's time the word *apology* simply meant "defense argument."

The middle dialogues are probably a combination of the ideas of the two men, as Plato's thoughts become increasingly dominant. Several of the final dialogues do away with Socrates altogether. It seems plain that Plato was emphasizing his own ideas. These ideas were the result of many years of teaching and thinking.

Plato was born in Athens, probably in 427 BCE. Some scholars put the actual date a year or two earlier. Both of his parents—Ariston, his father, and Perictione, his mother—came from long-established and important families. He had two brothers, Glaucon and Adeimantos. He also had a sister named Potone. It's likely that Plato was the youngest child. His father died when Plato was still relatively young. His mother quickly married a man named Pyrilampes. They had a son named Antiphon, Plato's half brother. The two boys were believed to be very close in age.

Plato was born in a turbulent era. Democracy had been established in Athens less than a century earlier. At that time, Greece didn't exist as a country. It consisted of hundreds of independent city-states. These city-states were also known as poleis. A polis consisted of the city itself and the surrounding countryside. *Polis* is at the root of such words as *police* and *politics*. It also appears in the names of several U.S. cities, such as Minneapolis, Indianapolis, and Annapolis.

The poleis had a few things in common. Their citizens spoke and wrote the same language. Their major gods were the same. They participated once every four years in the Olympic Games.

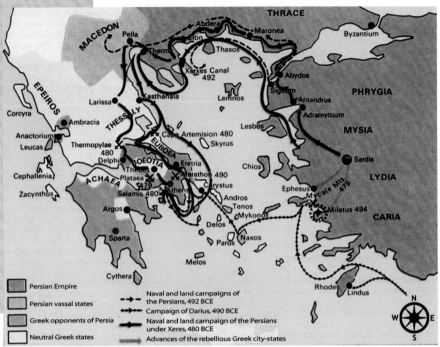

This map shows the major campaigns of the Persian Wars. Athens and Sparta put aside their differences and became allies. As a result, they were able to defeat the Persian threat. Yet the two sides soon split apart. They began the destructive Peloponnesian War in 431 BCE. It ended 27 years later with a Spartan victory. Neither side would ever regain its previous importance.

They also had many differences. It was hard for them to get along with each other. Wars among the city-states were common.

Persia, or modern-day Iran, controlled a vast empire. A little over sixty years before Plato was born, Persia was ruled by an emperor named Darius. He wanted to add the Greek city-states to the territories already under his control. He thought he could take advantage of their differences. It would be difficult for them to unite and defend themselves.

In 490 BCE, he launched an attack against Athens. An out-numbered army of Athenians defeated the Persians at the Battle of

Marathon. It was a stunning triumph. It showed the Greeks that they could stand up to the Persians.

Darius died a few years later. The new emperor, Xerxes, sent a much larger army and navy. This time the Greeks managed to put aside their differences. They followed the leadership of Athens and Sparta, another important Greek polis. The Greeks won a naval victory at Salamis in 480 BCE and a land battle at Plataea the following year. The Persian threat was ended.

Under the leadership of a statesman named Pericles, Athens entered what historians call the Golden Age. It was a time of extra-ordinary accomplishment in drama, literature, politics, architecture, and many other areas. Under Pericles' leadership, a vast civic building project began. It produced the Parthenon, one of the most famous buildings from ancient times. Millions of modern-day visitors from all over the world marvel at the ruins of the Parthenon every year.

Unfortunately, the Golden Age didn't last very long. With the Persian threat ended, the Greeks went back to their bickering. Athens and Sparta fought several relatively small wars. A much larger war broke out in 431 BCE. It is known as the Peloponnesian War. Many other poleis became involved. Some supported Athens, others supported Sparta. As a result, Plato grew up under the shadow of war. As a member of an important family, he would have received a good education in spite of the conflict. His schooling probably started when he was about seven years old.

One of the first requirements, then as now, was learning how to read and write. Mathematics was also important. Greeks were expected to know Homer's great epics the *Iliad* and the *Odyssey*. The stories were filled with moral lessons. Plato learned music. Music was an important part of public and private ceremonies. Youngsters were encouraged to learn how to play the lyre and to sing.

Education was more than mental. As he grew older, Plato would have worked out at a *gymnasion*. The Greek word *gymnos* means

An ancient Greek lyre, made from a turtle shell. The strings were stretched from the crossbar at the top to different points on the base. When they were plucked or strummed, they mde music.

"naked." Plato and his fellow students didn't wear any clothes while they exercised. The *gymnasion* included a running track. Unlike modern oval tracks, Greek tracks were about 200 yards long and very narrow. There was a pole at each end. When the runners reached the pole, they would grab it and use their momentum to spin around and head back in the other direction. The *gymnasion* probably also included jumping pits, fields for playing ball games and throwing the discus and javelin, and boxing and wrestling rings. Well-to-do Greek youths weren't wimps.

They couldn't afford to be. In time of war they were the main defenders of their polis. They formed an army of heavily armed and armored foot soldiers called hoplites. Middle- and lower-class Athenian citizens also had military obligations. They formed the crews of Athenian warships. These long and narrow ships, called triremes, were propelled by three banks of oars.

Some scholars believe that Plato was a good wrestler. He may have competed at the Olympics and other important Greek athletic contests. There is no record of his winning any of them.

No one knows when Plato met Socrates. It certainly happened by the time Plato was twenty, and probably much earlier. There is a story that Socrates had a dream shortly before meeting Plato. In the dream, a cygnet flew onto his lap. Soon the cygnet grew up and became a swan. The swan sang lovely songs. Dreams were very important to the Greeks. Socrates believed that Plato was the cygnet in his dream.

By the time Plato was in his late teens, the war had turned against the Athenians. Athenians began pointing fingers at one another. The democratic government was briefly overthrown in 411 BCE before being restored. Seven years later the war ended. Sparta won. Athens was defeated.

Again democracy was abolished. A group called the Thirty came to power. They killed some leaders of the democracy. They forced others to go into exile. The Thirty included Plato's uncles Critias and Charmides. They invited him to join them in the government. Young men with similar birth to Plato's and obvious talent usually went into politics. Plato was tempted.

"When I was young I expected, as the young often do, that as soon as I was grown up I should at once take part in the public life of the city," he explained many years later. "I supposed that in [the Thirty's] management of public affairs they would substitute justice for injustice in national life."[1]

He soon realized that he had supposed wrong. The Thirty asked Socrates to help arrest and execute a fellow citizen. He refused. Eight months after the Thirty had come to power, democracy was restored. But it was still on shaky ground. The next few years saw a series of abuses committed by the democratic majority on those who disagreed with them. They believed that these abuses were necessary to maintain their grip on power.

It was during this time that Socrates was put on trial and executed. Plato was horrified that a government could kill one of its most outstanding members.

"As I observed all this, and the men who were managing the city's affairs, and the laws and the customs then in force, the more I watched and the older I grew, the more difficult it seemed for me to follow out a policy of good government," he continued. "Finally I decided that all existing cities were badly governed—their constitutions were almost beyond remedy, unless some unpredictable force were brought to bear, aided by good fortune—and I was forced to say, in praise of true philosophy, that only by its help can political justice and the rights of the individual ever be discerned."[2]

The conclusion was logical: "The human race would therefore have no respite from its troubles, until either those who rightly and truly engaged in philosophy attained to political power, or those who had influence in cities through divine dispensation became true philosophers."[3]

In other words, the best form of government—indeed, the only form of government that would produce justice and public harmony—would be led by people who studied and loved wisdom.

Plato knew that people would have questions. What was wisdom? How would potential leaders go about learning how to be wise? What would prevent them from using their wisdom for their own ends?

Plato's most famous answers to those questions are in one of his dialogues. It is known as *The Republic*.

Xenophon

FYI
For Your Info

The Peloponnesian War ended in 404 BCE. Men from all over Greece who had fought—and fought well—for many years were left with little to do. That same year the Persian king Darius II died. His elder son, Artaxerxes II, succeeded him on the throne. Darius' younger son, Cyrus the Younger, decided that he was the rightful heir. In 401, Cyrus gathered a large force. It included 11,000 Greek hoplites, which were heavily armed infantrymen, and two thousand other lightly armed Greeks. This force would soon become immortal as the Ten Thousand. The men came from nine different poleis. Cyrus offered to pay the Greeks generously to help him overthrow his brother.

Cyrus was killed at the Battle of Cunaxa, near the Euphrates River in modern-day Iraq. Soon afterward, the leaders of the Greek soldiers were invited to attend a meeting conducted by Tissaphernes, the commander of Artaxerxes' army. The Greek leaders were all murdered. Tissaphernes ordered the Greek troops they commanded to lay down their arms and surrender.

The men were in a desperate situation. They were a thousand miles from home, surrounded by enemies. All of their leaders were dead. But they refused to give up. They decided to try to go home. To survive, it was essential for them to be unified. They had to overcome their allegiances to their particular poleis. One way of achieving this unity was to elect their own leaders. These new leaders included Xenophon, Plato's student.

Xenophon led 10,000 Greek soldiers from this enemy's land. They had to withstand almost constant attacks during the entire journey. No one was familiar with the territory they passed through. Their trek to the battlefield at Cunaxa had been over a much different and easier route. It would be too dangerous to return the same way. Nature didn't cooperate either. Much of the route was through mountains. The Greeks had little or no experience with the huge snowdrifts and raging snow-fed rivers they had to cross.

Despite the obstacles, almost all of the Greeks made it to safety. Xenophon wrote a book called *Anabasis* that tells what happened during the epic journey. It is one of the most famous works from the ancient world. Many scholars consider it to be the first true-life adventure story ever written.

Athenian democracy in action. Every citizen had
the right to express his opinion. During Plato's
time, citizenship (which included the right to
vote) extended only to free males who had
been born in the city.

CHAPTER
THREE

THE BEST FORM
OF GOVERNMENT

Plato lived through a lot of turbulence. He had personal experience of several forms of government. He didn't like any of them. He was thoroughly familiar with their shortcomings.

One of his concerns was disorder and disharmony among the citizens. Every polis had two classes—the rich and the poor. That tended to break down the sense of community that was necessary for the polis to survive. There were too many conflicts. Too many people were looking out for their own best interests.

Because of what had happened to Socrates, Plato was especially hard on democracies. An exchange in *The Republic* about democracy sounds very normal to most Americans.

"Well, aren't [citizens in a democracy] free men?" Socrates asks. "Isn't it a city full of freedom, and freedom of speech? Isn't there liberty in it for anyone to do anything he wants?"

"Yes, that's the reputation it has," [the other character] says.

"And where there is liberty, then obviously each person can arrange his own life within the city to whatever way pleases him."[1]

Plato didn't approve of thoughts like those. He believed that individuals were helpless on their own. They had to come together to help each other survive. The community was more important than the individuals who composed it. Allowing people to do what they wanted wasn't in the best interests of the community. Individual freedom had to give way to the greater good.

In Plato's view, freedom isn't the chance to do what one wants to. Freedom is what a person has to do because of his or her nature. For example, a good shoemaker might want to make a career change and become an actor. But he isn't a very good actor. For the good of society, he has to remain a shoemaker. That way society functions on its best level.

"More is produced—and it is better and more easily produced—when one person does a single task which is suited to his nature, and does it at the right time, keeping himself free from other tasks,"[2] Socrates explains, revealing what Plato believed.

Democracy had other faults. It was easy for the majority to impose its will on the minority. Another fault was even more troubling. Democracy was government by amateurs. Most people who were elected to public office had no training or ability in government. They were poorly equipped to handle their power.

Who should be in charge? For Plato, the answer was simple: people who had the training and the expertise to be good rulers. Only a few people fit those criteria.

Who were these people? According to Plato, most members of a community were best suited for occupations such as craftsmen, shopkeepers, and farmers. That was their role in society, and there was no shame in it. By performing their roles, they provided a solid economic basis for the community.

There were a few whose natural abilities made them qualified to serve as the city's "guardians." Most would be soldiers, offering protection for the community. Some of the guardians would rise beyond that level. They would provide overall leadership and government.

They couldn't rule selfishly, to advance their own interests. It was important that they rule for the good of everyone. To do this, they had to know what was good. To know what was good, they had to study philosophy. Eventually they would become what Plato called philosopher-kings.

For the system to succeed, two conditions are necessary. One is that economic power can't have any connection to political power. The other is that the philosopher-kings have to undergo decades of training.

Plato didn't want his guardians to have any private property or any money. Material possessions could lead to corruption and greed. The guardians would live together and eat together in simple barracks-style housing.

They wouldn't have their own families, either. It's natural for parents to want to advance the interests of their own children. But that couldn't happen in this ideal state. Instead, children would be immediately taken away from their parents when they were born. They would be raised together. They would never know who their parents were. Nor would the parents know the identity of their children.

This sounds very harsh. Yet in another way Plato was many centuries ahead of his time. Plato didn't like the state of marriage. He thought that it held women down. Capable women were welcome to become guardians. Few of his fellow citizens shared his opinion.

Another integral component was education. Everyone would receive a certain amount of schooling. It would end relatively early for most people. They would need to become contributing members of society as soon as possible.

The guardians would receive much more education than everyone else. At first, it would consist primarily of physical and music education to develop their bodies and their minds. There would be a series of levels. At the completion of each level, only the highest achievers would move on. Mathematics would become an especially important subject. The truths of mathematics are eternal. One plus one always equals two. The future rulers would need to know what is eternal and what is changing. Society and justice had to be founded on unchanging principles. The very best among the best would take control of the state when they were about fifty. They would administer it according to what they had learned through several decades of study.

Plato's ideal state may seem like a dictatorship. It isn't. Dictators seize power ruthlessly. They administer their states by fear. They execute people who don't agree with them. In Plato's Republic, there would be no cause for disagreements. Political murders would be unknown. Everyone would be happy.

Plato went beyond what most Greeks believed. They felt that every man had a right to some say in how he was governed. But Plato said they didn't. Only the philosopher-kings would have a say. They were true public servants. They would have no way of using their position to make money or to improve their lives. Their efforts would be devoted to making the polis run as smoothly as possible. They would be the only ones with the education to know what was good and what wasn't good.

Plato wasn't describing any polis that currently existed. He was looking for the best foundation of an ideal polis. It was literally a utopia, a place that doesn't exist.

In 387 BCE, Plato received an offer he couldn't refuse. It came from a place that very much did exist. It was an opportunity to see whether the principles he outlined in *The Republic* would work.

Women in Athens

Athenian women had two primary responsibilities. One was to produce children, especially boys who would carry on the family line. The other was to take care of the *oikos*, the household. *Oikos* is the root of our word *ecology*, which means to take care of the "household" of the earth.

To carry out these objectives, girls were normally married in their early teens. Their husbands were often at least twice as old. Many if not most marriages were arranged. Sometimes the bride and groom didn't even meet until their wedding day.

Once women were married, they were expected to spend most of their lives indoors. They would take care of the children, knit, and weave. Getting water provided one of the few opportunities to get out of the house. Women would go to the community wells. While waiting their turn to draw water, they could converse with their friends. Attending funerals provided another reason to appear in public. There were few others.

Athenian husbands, on the other hand, liked to spend the evenings away from home at dinner parties. They wouldn't have dreamed of taking their wives with them. It would have been too dangerous. The wives might be attracted to other men. Yet the men wanted female company at these parties. To fill this need, women called hetaerae would also attend. Most hetaerae were foreigners. Many had been captured in wars. They played the flute, danced, and laughed at the men's feeble jokes. Many could talk intelligently on a variety of subjects—something few husbands believed their wives were capable of doing.

Then as now, makeup was important. Researchers who dig up ancient homes have regularly found mirrors, perfume bottles, combs, and other beauty aids.

It is likely that women in other parts of Greece enjoyed more freedom than those in Athens. On the island of Lesbos, a woman named Sappho (who lived around 600 BCE) was a highly respected poet. Women in Sparta usually waited longer to marry than the Athenians. As a result, they were more mature. Their husbands respected them more. Unlike Athenian women, they could also inherit property.

Sappho

Italy

—— International boundary
★ National capital
● Southern Colonies

0	50	100
0	50	100 Miles

SWITZERLAND

AUSTRIA

FRANCE

YUGOSLAVIA

ITALY

Corsica

★ ROME

Adriatic Sea

Cumae
Pithekoussai ●
Poseidonia ●
Metapontion ●
Taras ●
Siris ●

Sardinia

Tyrrhenian Sea

Sybaris ●

Kroton ●

Ionian Sea

Lokroi Epizephyrioi ●

Zancle ●
Naxos ●
Reggio ●

Mediterranean Sea

Himera ●

Selinous ●
Sicily
Katane ●
Leontinoi ●
Megara Hybleaea ●
Syracuse ●

Akragas ●
Gela ●

Each dot on this modern map of Italy represents the location of an important ancient Greek colony. Plato visited many of them. The most important was at Syracuse. Plato hoped that his political ideas would take root there. Unfortunately, they didn't.

BIOGRAPHY FROM
ANCIENT CIVILIZATIONS
LEGENDS, FOLKLORE, AND STORIES OF ANCIENT WORLDS

CHAPTER
FOUR

PUTTING IDEAS INTO PRACTICE

While traveling among the Greek colonies in southern Italy, Plato was shocked by what he saw. The people lived, he wrote, "a life in which one gluts one's self twice a day and never sleeps alone at night, and indulges in all the practices that accompany this way of living. No man upon earth, engaging in such practices from his youth up, could ever, after forming these habits, attain to wisdom."[1]

Soon he received an invitation to visit the island of Sicily. It came from Dionysius, the ruler of the long-established Greek colony of Syracuse. Dionysius had a twenty-year-old brother-in-law named Dion. Plato believed that he could influence the young man. Perhaps Dion could become the philosopher-king Plato was seeking.

"Dion, who was always quick to learn, and was especially quick in understanding what I said then, listened more keenly and earnestly than any young man I have ever met, and decided to live the rest of his life in a manner different from most of the Italian and Sicilian Greeks, setting his heart upon virtue as being of more worth than pleasure, and all their soft, luxurious ways,"[2] Plato wrote.

Dion wasn't shy about expressing his enthusiasm for Plato's ideas. However, they conflicted with the lifestyle at Dionysius's court. Plato

31

himself apparently made some negative comments to Dionysius. Not surprisingly, Dionysius wanted him gone. According to several stories, Dionysius put him on a ship heading back for Athens. He told the captain to sell Plato into slavery before reaching the city. Fortunately, a friend of Plato's recognized him in the slave market and paid his ransom.

When Plato returned to Athens, he founded what most scholars regard as the first university in the Western world. Known as the Academy, it was located in a grove of trees dedicated to a hero named Akademos.

The school attracted people from all over Greece. Plato didn't charge tuition, but he was careful about whom he admitted. Students had to show that they were eager to learn. Classes were somewhat informal. Plato would stroll slowly through the school, either lecturing or reading from the dialogues he had written. Banquets that lasted until dawn were fairly common. They served two purposes: to allow the students to bond with each other, and to allow free discussion of the issues that Plato had presented.

Plato settled into a comfortable routine. Then in 367 BCE, his old friend Dion asked him to come back to Syracuse. Dionysius the Elder had just died. He had been succeeded by his son, Dionysius the Younger. Dion said that Plato had had a profound effect on his own life. Perhaps he could have the same effect on the new king. If he succeeded, Syracuse would be much better off.

Plato had his doubts, but he felt he had an obligation to try. He had devoted most of his life to studying the principles of government. "If anyone were ever to try to realize our theories about laws and constitution, an attempt must be made now," he wrote. "I set out from home . . . chiefly for the sake of self-respect, fearing the shame of seeming to myself to be nothing more than a mere man of words, who would never set his hand to any deed."[3]

The National Academy in Athens is the modern version of Plato's Academy. Socrates and Plato are seated in the front. On the two columns are Apollo, god of clear thinking, and Athena, goddess of wisdom.

The project was a flop. Dionysius the Younger wasn't a good student. He also became convinced that Dion was trying to overthrow him. He forced Dion into exile. For a while Plato was under suspicion as well. Finally Dionysius allowed Plato to return home. Dion joined him at the Academy.

Five years later Dionysius invited Plato to come back. Plato turned him down. He said he was too old to travel. The following year Dionysius sent another invitation. This time he sent the invitation with a man whom Plato respected. Dionysius claimed he was more interested in philosophy. He also said that if Plato didn't come, he wouldn't allow Dion to come back from exile.

Despite his previous lack of success, Plato agreed to make the trip. Maybe Dionysius was sincere this time. It didn't take him long to realize that this venture wouldn't be any more successful than the first two. Dionysius still wasn't interested in studying philosophy. He made Dion stay in exile and took over all of his property. Again Plato asked to go home.

Plato still wasn't finished with the politics of Syracuse. He attended the Olympic Games there in 360 BCE. Dion also attended. He asked Plato to help him overthrow Dionysius. Plato decided to keep out of the situation. Several years later, Dion succeeded in driving out Dionysius; but his term was short. Dion was assassinated in 354 BCE, and Dionysius the Younger was returned to power.

Plato spent the rest of his life in comfort and security at the Academy. He never gave up believing that his ideal state was possible. The philosopher-kings would rule on the basis of their wisdom and their knowledge. They would know what was right and wrong, so they would have no need for laws.

Plato's experiences in Syracuse probably affected his thinking. He became increasingly aware that it would be difficult to achieve his ideal state. One of his last works was *The Laws*. In it, he described a "second-best" state, which would be under the rule of law. It wouldn't be as good as being ruled by a philosopher-king, but it would be better than being ruled by men who had no training in government or by tyrants such as either Dionysius.

Plato died in 347 BCE. He was buried in a garden near the Academy. His ideas would never perish.

Greek Colonies

Historians believe that the Greeks began their polis system sometime in the ninth century BCE. They began exporting the system soon afterward. Settlers from many poleis began founding colonies in other parts of the Mediterranean. These colonies were known as *apoikiai*, or "away homes." The polis from which a colony originated was called a metropolis, or "mother city." The colonists were most active in Italy. Today, some of the best-preserved Greek ruins can be found in Italy.

Greek ruins in Italy

Some colonies were founded by "losers." If a polis lost a war, its survivors might look for another location where they could live in peace. On other occasions, a polis would be torn apart by a civil war. The winners would remain in control of the existing polis. The others would leave and establish a new polis far away from their former fellow citizens.

Another reason for establishing colonies was population growth. A polis might eventually have so many people that its resources couldn't adequately support everyone. A select group would set out and establish itself in a new location.

One obvious reason for founding colonies was superior conditions for growing crops. Even today, much of Greece is rocky and relatively infertile. That was not the case in some regions of Italy. Lava and ash from nearby volcanoes enriched the soil, producing lush crops.

Still another colonizing purpose was economic. Colonies helped to advance trade with other countries. They were much closer to major markets in these countries, so it was easier to conduct business there.

Syracuse was one of the most important Greek colonies. It was founded on the island of Sicily—probably around 730 BCE—by settlers from the polis of Corinth. In 415 BCE, Athens decided to attack Syracuse. It was a disaster. Two years later, many Athenians were killed in battle. Even more were captured. Nearly all of the captives were worked to death in the marble quarries near the city. The result was a serious weakening of Athens' military power during the Peloponnesian War. The city never really recovered from its horrendous losses.

A detail from "The School of Athens" (see page 41 for the entire painting). Plato (on the left) points upward to illustrate his emphasis on the life of the mind. His most famous student, Aristotle, has a different opinion. He gestures downward. This illustrates his belief that the real world is most important.

CHAPTER
FIVE

AFTER PLATO

Historian Donald Kagan believes Plato may have been too harsh in his judgment on democracy. "Starting with the fuller democracy instituted by Ephialtes and Pericles from 461, we discover an almost unbroken, orderly regime that lasted 140 years," he writes. "Through many years . . . the Athenian democracy persisted and showed a restraint and moderation rarely equaled by any regime."[1]

Plato thought that Sparta had a much better form of government than Athens. Sparta's primary purpose was to create excellent warriors. Everyone in Sparta directed his or her efforts toward that goal. There was little room for individuality. In the short term, it may have appeared that Plato's judgment was correct. Sparta did overcome Athens. During much of Plato's adult life, Sparta was the dominant Greek polis.

Yet the Greek historian Thucydides, who lived about the same time as Plato, made an astonishing prediction. "Suppose the city of Sparta to be deserted, and nothing left but the temples and the ground plan, distant ages would be very unwilling to believe that the power of the [Spartans] was at all equal to their fame," he wrote, "whereas, if the same fate befell the Athenians, the ruins of Athens would strike

Thucydides is one of the most famous historical writers of all time. His description of the Peloponnesian War—a war that tore the Greek city-states apart—is a classic both of history and of literature. Thucydides was no armchair adventurer. He was one of the most important military leaders in Athens and wrote from firsthand experience.

the eye, and we should infer their power to have been twice as great as it really was."[2]

Visitors to Greece have discovered how correctly Thucydides predicted the future. Most of them arrive in Athens. They spend much of their time touring the city's ancient ruins. They are especially impressed with the Parthenon. Though Sparta still exists, hardly any tourists go there. There is almost nothing of interest. It is simply a sleepy Greek town.

In other areas, Plato's legacy is much more secure. His Academy lasted for nearly a thousand years. It influenced many political leaders and other influential people.

His name endures in the term *platonic love*. This kind of relationship is a "meeting of the minds" between a man and woman. They enjoy talking with each other. They care deeply for each other. But there is no physical attraction.

The Parthenon in Athens is probably the best-known building from ancient times. It lasted in its original form for nearly 2,000 years. Early in the sixteenth century, it was being used to store ammunition. A cannon shell set off the ammunition. Most of the building was destroyed. What exists today is largely a reconstruction using the material that could be salvaged.

One of the more unusual legacies relates to Atlantis. Plato describes the city in two of his dialogues. He was the first person to write about it. He was far from the last. The whereabouts of Atlantis is still a mystery.

Plato was a very important influence on the development of the Christian church. Early Christianity was almost at war with "pagan influences" such as the Greek gods. Yet many important Christian writers read Plato. Plato believed that there was a divine purpose to life. So did these Christians. His beliefs helped shape their thinking.

Perhaps his supreme influence is summed up by Albert North Whitehead, a twentieth-century philosopher. He wrote that European philosophy is "a series of footnotes to Plato"[3]—meaning Plato was the first truly important philosopher. Plato's influence has remained strong through the present time.

One of the greatest "footnotes" was Aristotle, who entered the Academy at about the time that Plato made his second trip to Syracuse. He stayed at the Academy until Plato died twenty years later. By then it was obvious that he was Plato's best student. Many people believed that he would take over the Academy.

That wasn't to be. Plato's nephew Speusippus became the head. Aristotle left the Academy and a few years later became the personal tutor of Alexander the Great. Later he began his own school, the Lyceum.

It is likely that Plato and Aristotle had some disagreements while Plato was still alive. Aristotle was too independent a thinker to simply follow Plato's teachings.

Their main difference was about what was most real. Plato proposed the theory of Forms. He didn't trust the human senses. He believed what people perceived wasn't real. It was a copy of an ideal Form. The purpose of philosophy was to learn about these ideal Forms.

Aristotle disagreed. He believed what we perceived was real. He made many careful observations and recorded them. In many ways Aristotle was the first scientist. For nearly 2,000 years, people accepted his conclusions. It has only been in the last few centuries that his influence began to be reduced. Scientists gained access to instruments Aristotle never dreamed about. They have been able to make much more accurate observations than he had been able to.

Renaissance painter Raphael illustrates their differences in *The School of Athens*. Plato and Aristotle are the central figures. Plato points upward, toward heaven. Aristotle gestures downward, toward the earth.

The School of Athens *is one of the most famous paintings by Raphael. It was probably completed about 1510. The work is centered around Plato and Aristotle. Other important scholars are also portrayed, including Xenophon, Socrates, Xenocrates, Theophrastus, Pythagoras, Parmenides, Euclid, Ptolemy, and Zoroaster. Raphael put himself in the painting, too. He's seated at the far right, peeking around Sodoma, the man in the white.*

Yet Plato's ultimate goal was to discover the best way for people to act among themselves and in society. The thinkers who came after him may disagree with his conclusions, but their conclusions often start with Plato. He was a man who believed that nothing was more important than knowing what was right. He believed if people knew what is right, then they would do what is right.

FYI
For Your Info

Atlantis

Plato wrote about a sunken city known as Atlantis in his dialogues *Timaeus* and *Critias*. Since then, somewhere between 2,000 and 10,000 books have been written about Atlantis. Countless numbers of magazine articles and several movies have taken Atlantis as their theme. In most stories, Atlantis is an island or even a continent.

As described by Plato, the city was established many years before by Poseidon, the Greek god of the sea. It was located on an island west of the Pillars of Hercules (two promontories that lie on either side of the entrance to the Strait of Gibraltar). The city consisted of a series of circles within circles. The land was fertile. The citizens lived in peace.

Then about 9,000 years before Plato began writing, the city became corrupt. Its soldiers began attacking other countries. The gods decided to destroy Atlantis. A flood overwhelmed it, and it sank beneath the sea. There was nothing to show where it had been.

It may have been the end of Atlantis, but it was only the beginning of its story. As author Richard Ellis notes, "It is a story so powerful that it has lasted solely on the basis of its own merits, passed along, often by word of mouth, for two and a half millennia, and today, in an era characterized by technological marvels like atomic energy and the Internet, the legend of Atlantis still thrives."[4]

In recent years, explorers have embarked on extensive, expensive expeditions to try to locate the sunken city. Many people have tried to explain what happened to it. One man even claimed that the city flew out of the ocean and became the moon.

A more down-to-earth explanation has also been suggested. Sometime around 1500 BCE, a powerful volcanic eruption vaporized much of the Greek island of Santorini. It created a massive earthquake and tidal wave. The tidal wave swooped down on the island of Crete. It destroyed the city of Knossos. Knossos had been the center of a long-lasting civilization. Like Atlantis, its inhabitants had been peaceful. Then the city was gone.

Plato probably wrote his "Atlantis" dialogues in roughly 350 BCE. He would have known about the Santorini eruption. Its date of 1500 is an approximation. He might have written that it took place about 900 years before he wrote, rather than 9,000. Perhaps he accidentally added an extra zero. Or his calculations could have been mistranslated. In any event, the destruction of Knossos remains the most likely "real-life" model for Atlantis.

Chronology

(All dates BCE)

427   Plato is born in Athens

407   Possible date of meeting his teacher Socrates

399   Socrates is forced to commit suicide by drinking hemlock

387   Travels to Syracuse to train a philosopher-king; on his way back is almost sold into slavery

386   Returns to Athens; founds the Academy

367   Travels to Syracuse again to meet Dionysius the Younger; Aristotle becomes his student at the Academy

362   Makes final trip to Syracuse

347   Dies in Athens

Selected Works

Early	**Middle**	**Late**
Apology	*Cratylus*	*Critias*
Charmides	*Meno*	*Laws*
Crito	*Parmenides*	*Philebus*
Euthydemus	*Phaedo*	*Sophist*
Euthyphro	*Phaedrus*	*Statesman*
Gorgias	*Republic*	*Timaeus*
Hippias Major	*Symposium*	
Hippias Minor	*Theaetetus*	
Ion		
Laches		
Lysis		
Protagoras		

Timeline in History

(All dates BCE)

536 Persian emperor Cyrus II releases the Jews from their captivity in Babylon; they return to Israel.

519 Xerxes, the future Persian emperor, is born.

509 Rome expels its last king and becomes a republic.

507 Athens becomes the world's first democracy.

493 Athenian leader Pericles is born.

490 A heavily outnumbered Athenian army defeats the Persians at the Battle of Marathon.

480 A fleet of Greek ships defeats Persians at the Battle of Salamis.

479 The Greek victory in the Battle of Plataea ends the Persian threat.

470 The philosopher Socrates is born.

460 The famous Greek physician Hippocrates is born; even today many medical professionals take the Hippocratic Oath, a code of ethics.

448 Pericles undertakes an extensive building project that includes the Parthenon.

431 The Peloponnesian War begins.

429 Pericles dies.

423 Aristophanes' play *The Clouds*, which makes fun of Socrates, debuts.

413 The Athenians suffer a crippling defeat at the Greek colony of Syracuse on the island of Sicily.

404 The Peloponnesian War ends, with Sparta victorious over Athens.

403 The Thirty Tyrants are deposed after eight months of rule in Athens.

384 The philosopher Aristotle is born.

356 Alexander the Great is born.

338 King Philip II of Macedon defeats a combined Greek army at Chaeronea.

335 In Athens, Aristotle founds the Lyceum, a rival school to Plato's Academy.

323 Alexander the Great dies.

322 Aristotle dies.

146 Rome completes its conquest of Greece by winning the Battle of Corinth; Greece becomes a Roman province.

BIOGRAPHY FROM
ANCIENT CIVILIZATIONS
LEGENDS, FOLKLORE, AND STORIES OF ANCIENT WORLDS

Chapter Notes

Chapter 1   Sentenced to Die

1. Aristophanes, *The Clouds,* translated by William Arrowsmith, in *Four Plays by Aristophanes* (New York: Meridian Books, 1994), p. 33.

2. Ibid., p. 34.

3. Ibid., p. 36.

4. Plato, "Apology," translated by Benjamin Jowett, in *Selected Dialogues of Plato* (New York: The Modern Library, 2000), pp. 301–02.

5. Ibid., p. 311.

6. Ibid., p. 313.

7. Ibid., p. 318.

8. Plato, "Phaedo," translated by Benjamin Jowett in *The Portable Plato,* edited by Scott Buchanan (New York: Penguin Books, 1977), p. 273.

9. Ibid., p. 277.

Chapter 2   Growing Up a Thinker

1. Plato, "Seventh Letter," translated by R. S. Bluck, in R. S. Bluck, *Plato's Life and Thought* (Boston: The Beacon Press, 1951), pp. 152–153.

2. Ibid., p. 154.

3. Ibid., pp. 154–155.

Chapter 3   The Best Form of Government

1. Plato, *The Republic,* translated by Tom Griffith, edited by G.R.F. Ferrari (New York: Cambridge University Press, 2000), p. 269.

2. Ibid., p. 50.

Chapter 4   Putting Ideas into Practice

1. Plato, "Seventh Letter," translated by R. S. Bluck, in R. S. Bluck, *Plato's Life and Thought* (Boston: The Beacon Press, 1951), p. 155.

2. Ibid., p. 156.

3. Ibid., p. 157.

Chapter 5   After Plato

1. Donald Kagan, *Pericles of Athens and the Birthplace of Democracy* (New York: The Free Press, 1991), p. 61.

2. Oliver Taplin, *Greek Fire: The Influence of Ancient Greece on the Modern World* (New York: Atheneum, 1990), pp. 207–208.

3. Bernard Williams, *Plato: The Invention of Philosophy* (New York: Routledge, 1999), p. 1.

4. Richard Ellis, *Imagining Atlantis* (New York: Alfred A. Knopf, 1998), p. 5.

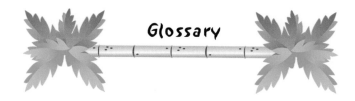

BIOGRAPHY FROM

ANCIENT CIVILIZATIONS

LEGENDS, FOLKLORE, AND STORIES OF ANCIENT WORLDS

Glossary

anus	(AY-nus)—lower opening of the large intestine through which the body's waste products are expelled.
benefactor	(BEH-nuh-fak-tur)—a person who does good things for others.
cygnet	(SIG-net)—a young swan.
dialogue	(DYE-uh-log)—a written literary work that recounts a conversation between two or more people.
dispensation	(dis-pen-SAY-shun)—formal authorization or permission.
flatulent	(FLAT-choo-lent)—causing or having intestinal gas.
impiety	(im-PYE-uh-tee)—not respecting or honoring the established God or gods.
poleis	(POE-lase)—plural of *polis*.
polis	(POE-liss)—a Greek city-state, consisting of a central town or city and the surrounding countryside.
regime	(ruh-JEEM)—the government that is in power.

Further Reading

For Young Adults

Balit, Christina. *Atlantis: The Legend of a Lost City*. New York: Henry Holt, 2000.

Bowen, Richard, and Iassen Ghiuselev. *Socrates: Greek Philosopher*. Broomall, Penn.: Mason Crest Publishers, 2002.

Jones, John Ellis. *Ancient Greece*. New York: Warwick Press, 1983.

Kurtti, Jeff. *The Mythical World of Atlantis: Theories of the Lost Empire from Plato to Disney*. New York: Disney Editions, 2001.

Pearson, Anne. *Eyewitness: Ancient Greece*. New York: DK Publishing, 2004.

Robinson, Charles Alexander Jr. *Ancient Greece*. New York: Franklin Watts, 1984.

Works Consulted

Aristophanes. *Four Plays by Aristophanes*. Translated by William Arrowsmith, Richmond Lattimore and Douglass Parker. New York: Meridian Books, 1994.

Bluck, R. S. *Plato's Life and Thought*. Boston: The Beacon Press, 1951.

Dersin, Denise (editor). *What Life Was Like at the Dawn of Democracy: Classical Athens 525–322 BC*. Alexandria, Va.: Time-Life Books, 1997.

Ellis, Richard. *Imagining Atlantis*. New York: Alfred A. Knopf, 1998.

Hare, R. M. "Plato." *Greek Philosophers*. Oxford, United Kingdom: Oxford University Press, 1999.

Kagan, Donald. *The Great Dialogue: History of Greek Political Thought from Homer to Polybius*. Westport, Conn.: Greenwood Press, Publishers, 1986.

———. *Pericles of Athens and the Birthplace of Democracy*. New York: The Free Press, 1991.

Plato. *The Portable Plato*. Translated by Benjamin Jowett. Edited by Scott Buchanan. New York: Penguin Books, 1977.

Plato. *The Republic*. Translated by Tom Griffith. Edited by G.R.F. Ferrari. New York: Cambridge University Press, 2000.

Pradeau, Jean-François. *Plato and the City: A New Introduction to Plato's Political Thought*. Translated by Janet Lloyd. Exeter, England: University of Exeter Press, 2002.

Robinson, Dave, and Judy Groves. *Introducing Plato*. Cambridge, England: Icon Books, 2000.

Taplin, Oliver. *Greek Fire: The Influence of Ancient Greece on the Modern World*. New York: Atheneum, 1990.

Taylor, C.C.W. *Socrates: A Very Short Introduction*. Oxford, England: Oxford University Press, 1998.

Williams, Bernard. *Plato: The Invention of Philosophy*. New York: Routledge, 1999.

On the Internet

Dunkle, Roger. *Brooklyn College Core Curriculum Series: "Apology."*
http://depthome.brooklyn.cuny.edu/classics/dunkle/studyguide/apology.htm

Krystek, Lee. *The Lost Continent of Atlantis*.
http://www.unmuseum.org/atlantis.htm

Linder, Douglas. *The Trial of Socrates*.
http://www.law.umkc.edu/faculty/projects/ftrials/socrates/socrates.HTM

New Banner Institute. *School of Athens*.
http://www.newbanner.com/AboutPic/athena/raphael/nbi_ath4.html

Suzanne, Bernard. *Plato and His Dialogues*.
http://plato-dialogues.org/life.htm

Thompson, James C. *Women in the Ancient World*.
http://www.womenintheancientworld.com

Index